After 23 years of managing, developing, testing, and supporting unix / linux based software projects, I've found that unix shell scripting and awk are powerful, but under-appreciated tools that make a dramatic difference.

They are a classic example of working smarter instead of harder.

The unix philosophy is to take small scripts that do one thing well, and connect them together through redirection and pipes. This way, you can rapidly build and prototype complex applications with a minimum amount of risk.

With today's hardware and chips, 90% of the time, interpreted unix scripts will perform as efficiently as code written in higher level languages – such as java.

The difference is that , with unix scripts, you cut out about 80-90% of the lines of code, and have something that can easily be maintained and supported.

Even if you still want to code in a higher level language, unix shell scripting is invaluable for support functions – such as moving around files, parsing log files, etc.

An analyst or support person who uses the topics and examples in this book to master scripting can save him or herself literally hundreds of hours – especially when dealing with repetitive tasks with many lines of data.

Examples of this would include running a unix command on a thousand different files, or generating database insert statements for 500 rows of a spreadsheet.

How To Use This Book

The best way to use this book is to study the sample code, type it into a unix window, and run it. Then – tear them apart, combine commands, try different options. Experiment, experiment, experiment! Try to automate and solve real issues that come up in your daily work. Also, make up data files and example problems to solve.

Not Just For Unix and Linux Systems

Unix Shell Scripting and Awk can also be used on Macs (which actually run on unix) and pc's.

For Macs, just open a terminal window, and you have full access to unix.

For pc's, there are many free and open source versions of awk and unix tools.

Assumptions

This book assumes that you can access a korn shell (ksh) and have some basic unix command knowledge (i.e. can change directories, list files, basic use of the vi editor, etc.)

Now, let's get started!

Table of Contents

The Unix Shell For Loop

If you are a programmer or engineer working in a unix or linux environment, you will probably find the shell 'for' loop to be a handy tool for automating command line tasks.

Here are three examples of the 'for' loop. All the commands are in italics and should be entered on the command line, followed by a carriage return.
Note that, after entering the initial 'for' line, you will get the secondary unix prompt, which is usually a ">".

1. Rename all ".old" files in the current directory to ".bak":

```
for i in *.old
do
j=`echo $i|sed 's/old/bak/'`
mv $i $j
done
```

Here, we looped thru all files with extension ".old", setting the variable "i" to be the file name we are currently looping thru. Then, between the "do" and "done", we have the body of the loop. On each pass, we echo the file name ("i") to the unix stream editor sed. Sed replaces the "old" with "bak" (so file "a.old" becomes "a.bak"), and saves the changed name to variable "j". Then, we use the unix move (mv) command to rename the original file (ex. a.old) to the new file (a.bak).

2. Change all instances of "yes" to "no" in all ".txt" files in the current directory. Back up the original files to ".bak".

```
for i in *.txt
do
j=`echo $i|sed 's/txt/bak/'`
```

6

```
   mv $i $j
    sed 's/yes/no/' $j > $i
   done
```

In this case, we rename each file from ".txt" to ".bak". Additionally, we use sed a second time, on the **contents** of the original file (now with a ".bak" extension) and save the modified text back to the original name (with ".txt").

3. Loop thru a text file containing possible file names.
If the file is readable, print the first line, otherwise print an error message:

```
for i in `cat file_list.txt`
 do
     if test -r $i
     then
         echo "Here is the first line of file: $i"
         sed 1q $i
     else
         echo "file $i cannot be open for reading."
     fi
 done
```

Here, we loop thru the results of a command (in this case "cat"), rather than looping thru files in the directory. We also use an if statement with the "test" command to test for a condition (in this case, whether the file is readable).

Awk, Nawk, Gawk

A lot of the awk examples I will share have been done on a Sun Solaris System.

Sun keeps the original version of awk on its systems. This version is very basic, and does not contain many of the features in the current standard version of awk.

Sun systems carry this new version as "nawk" (for new awk).

On other systems, like AIX, HPUX, Linux, etc. the standard version is called "awk".

Finally, the GNU project has an awk version called Gawk, which is free and available for all systems, including windows.

For almost all my examples, all the awks (except the Sun awk) will work.

So, if you see me type "nawk ..." and you are on another system besides Sun, you can change the nawk to awk.

Making Unix Shell Variables Upper and Lower Case

When writing unix ksh programs, you can use the built-in typeset command to make variables upper and lower case only.

typeset -l sets a variable to be lowercase only. If uppercase characters are assigned, they are automatically converted to lowercase.

Example:

[541]-> typeset -l small

[542]-> small="BIG"

[543]-> echo $small

big

typeset -u sets a variable to be uppercase only. Any lowercase chars are converted to uppercase.

Example:

[544]-> typeset -u big

[545]-> big="i am tiny"

[546]-> echo $big

I AM TINY

Unix Shell Variable Editing Hacks

The unix korn shell (ksh) has some neat tricks for editing variables:

${variable#pattern} will return *variable* with the smallest possible *pattern* removed from the front.

```
[586]-> t="/etc/tmp/foo.c"
[587]-> echo ${t#*/}
etc/tmp/foo.c
```

${variable##pattern} will return *variable* with the largest possible *pattern* removed from the front.
```
[586]-> t="/etc/tmp/foo.c"
[587]-> echo ${t##*/}
foo.c
```

${variable%pattern} will return *variable* with the smallest possible *pattern* removed from the back.

```
[589]-> t=foo.c.bak
[590]-> echo ${t%.*}
foo.c
```

${variable%%pattern} will return *variable* with the largest possible *pattern* removed from the back.

```
[589]-> t=foo.c.bak
[590]-> echo ${t%%.*}
foo
```

I always remember that # slashes from the front, and % from the back, because # comes before % on the keyboard.

The % can be handy for scripts that move files to back up versions.

i.e. If f = "sample.txt", you can move it to "sample.bak" with: **mv $f ${f%.txt}.bak**

Read-Only Unix Shell Variables

You can use typeset -r to make variables in a ksh script be read-only. This effectively makes them constants, which can no longer be modified.

For example:

```
[550]-> pi=3.14159

[551]-> echo $pi

3.14159

[552]-> typeset -r pi

[553]-> pi=45

ksh: pi: is read only

[554]-> echo $pi

3.14159
```

Don't Be Square, Part 1

Let's look at an awk program called "square". It takes a number as an argument, and prints out
its square.

Here is the run of the program:

```
[628]-> square
Usage: square number

[629]-> square 4
The square of 4.00 is: 16.00
```

Let's look at the program, which is in a file called "square" on my system:

```
#! /usr/bin/nawk -f

BEGIN {

if (ARGC <2)
{
printf ("Usage: square number\n")
exit 1
}

printf ("The square of %.2f is: %.2f\n", ARGV[1], ARGV[1] ^2)


}
```

The first line, "#!...", tells unix what command to use to run this file. By putting this line in the file, I can just type "square *number*" to run it. If this line was not there, I would have to type "nawk -f square *number*" to run the file. If you were using gawk on windows, for example, you would have to type "gawk -f square *number*" in your DOS window.

The next thing to notice is that the program is blocked into a section called

"BEGIN". By default, awk tries to read a file or input stream, and apply its commands to each line. Commands in a BEGIN block are executed once, before any input is processed. If your awk program only has a BEGIN block, then awk works just like a standard procedural language. It executes the commands top to bottom.

The "if" statement executes if there are less than 2 arguments (the program name + the number). If so, it prints the usage information, and exits with a status code of 1. The unix convention is that a program returns 0 if execution was successful, or else a non-zero error code.

If we make it past the argument check, the program prints the square and exits (with a default return code of 0).

One of the authors of awk was also the author of C and unix. Thus, awk uses a lot of C commands and syntax. One of the features of awk is the C printf statement (awk also has a simpler print statement).

The printf command arguments consist of the message in quotes (with formatters like %f for variables) and a list of any variables used. Printf does not automatically put a new line at the end of the message, so the user must insert a backslash n for a carriage return.

In the second printf statement we use %.2f as the formatter. %f is floating point, while %c is a character, %s is a string, and %d is an integer. The .2 says that we want 2 decimal places.

A lot of times, a simple print statement will do, but printf gives you a lot of control for output.

Don't Be Square, Part 2

Here is another squares AWK program. This one prints the squares from 1 to 10.

Here is the run:

```
[721]-> ./squares

Squares from 1 to 10
Number   Square
------   ------
1        1
2        4
3        9
4        16
5        25
6        36
7        49
8        64
9        81
10       100
```

Here is the code:

```
#! /usr/bin/nawk -f
BEGIN
{
  printf ("\nSquares from 1 to 10")
  printf ("\nNumber\tSquare\n")
  printf ("------\t------\n")

  for (i=1; i<=10; i++)
      printf ("%d\t%d\n", i, i^2)
}
```

Here, the new thing is the for loop. This is a standard C for loop. There are 3 parts to the for clause (spearated by ;s). The first part initializes i to 1, the second part says that the loop should only be done while i is less than or equal to 10, and the third part says to increment i by 1 after each execution of the body of the loop. In this case, the loop is just the next line, since I did not enclose any statements in brackets.

Don't Be Square, Part 3

This third "squares" example will show how to read in a file of numbers to be squared, while still using standard procedural execution, with the script enclosed in a BEGIN block.

Here is the file of numbers we will use for input:

```
[754]-> cat tmpfile
18
3
23
125
```

The run will look like this:

```
[755]-> square_file tmpfile
The square of 18 is: 324
The square of 3 is: 9
The square of 23 is: 529
The square of 125 is: 15625
```

Here is the script:

```
#! /usr/bin/nawk -f

BEGIN {
    if (ARGC < 2)
    {
      printf ("Usage: %s file\n",ARGV[0])
      exit 1
    }

    while ( getline < ARGV[1])
      printf ("The square of %d is: %d\n", $1, $1 ^ 2 )
  }
```

Here we see that awk uses the standard while loop: The printf statement is executed
as long as the body of the while loop is true.

The while loop body, however, consists of a command unique to awk: the getline.

A good way to think of getline is to think of it as a unix filter. Invoking Getline retrieves and returns the next line from standard input. Just like a filter, however, getline can have its input redirected from a file or piped in from a command (which we will see in the next "squared" example).

In this case, getline reads from the file named by the first argument. This while loop will go thru all the lines in the file, until getline gets to the end of the file, and returns 0 (non-true).

Don't Be Square, Part 4

Now, we will add a twist to the square_file program from the last example. We will still use the same input file

```
[771]-> cat tmpfile
18
3
23
125
```

But, now, our numbers to be squared are displayed sorted, from lowest to highest:

```
[774]-> ./square_file2 tmpfile
The square of 3 is: 9
The square of 18 is: 324
The square of 23 is: 529
The square of 125 is: 15625
```

Here is the code:

```
#! /usr/bin/nawk -f

BEGIN {
    if (ARGC < 2)
    {
      printf ("Usage: %s file\n",ARGV[0])
      exit 1
    }

    while ( "sort -n "ARGV[1] | getline)
      printf ("The square of %d is: %d\n", $1, $1 ^ 2 )
    }
```

Notice that the only thing that has changed is the *getline* statement in the while loop. Last time, we redirected the argument to *getline*, so it was opened as a file.

Now, we made a unix command string (to numerically sort the file). By piping the string into *getline*, awk executes it in unix, and puts the output into getline.

The interesting thing here is that getline executes the command just once, on its first use. After that, until a close("sort -n "ARGV[1]) is used, or the script ends, the pipe stays open and each call to "sort -n "ARGV[1] getline returns the next line in the file.

Before, the while loop ended when getline reached the end of the file. In this case, the while loop ends when getline gets to the end of the pipe contents.

Awk Basics

Some languages, such as basic and C, are procedural - the program executes once, top to bottom. Languages like java are object-oriented - the program is written as a series of objects which interact with each other.

Awk is an iterative language. An awk program consists of pattern {actions } blocks. Awk automatically loops thru all standard input, parses the input into records and fields, and applies the action(s) to any records that match the corresponding pattern.

By default, one record = one line of input. The variable NR is the current record number (i.e. line number). In advanced usage, the user can redefine the record to span multiple lines.

Each record is split into one or more fields. The default separator is white space (blanks, spaces, tabs). Each field in a record is denoted by a "$" sign and number (i.e. $4 is the fourth field on the current record).

Patterns and actions are optional: a pattern with no actions will print any lines that match the pattern. Action(s) with no pattern will be done for all lines. An awk program with no pattern or action will just loop thru standard input and do nothing.

There are 2 special patterns: BEGIN and END. Any actions in a BEGIN block are executed once, before standard input is looped through. Actions in the END block are done once, after standard input is processed.

The BEGIN block also has the special feature that, if it is used in an awk program with no standard input, it makes awk into a regular procedural language. We have been using awk this way in the "Don't Be Square" examples. An awk program with no BEGIN block and no standard input will just hang.

Here are some example pattern/action blocks:

/^The/ {print $1} Print the first field of the line if the line starts with "The"

$2==5 \{x = 12\}$ Set variable x equal to 12 if the second field of the line is 5

NR<=32 If the line is one of the first 32, we will print it (the default action)

{Name[NR]=$4} For all lines (default), store field 4 in array element Name[line number]

Don't Be Square, Part 5

In this last Squares example, we will rewrite the awk program from "Don't Be Square, Part 3" into awk's iterative style.

This was the procedural program we had written to loop through a file of numbers and square them:

```
#! /usr/bin/nawk -f

BEGIN {
    if (ARGC < 2)
    {
      printf ("Usage: %s file\n",ARGV[0])
      exit 1
    }

     while ( getline < ARGV[1])
        printf ("The square of %d is: %d\n", $1, $1 ^ 2 )
   }
```

Now, we will write the program using the built-in iteration of awk:

```
#! /usr/bin/nawk -f

BEGIN {
    if (ARGC < 2)
    {
      printf ("Usage: %s file\n",ARGV[0])
      exit 1
      }
    }

    {printf ("The square of %d is: %d\n", $1, $1 ^ 2 )}
```

Notice that, instead of having the whole program in the BEGIN block, we have moved the *printf* statement that does the squaring into its own *{} block* which has no pattern. This means that the *printf* statement will be executed for each line in standard input. We do not have to explicitly loop with *while* and *getline*.

There is a difference between the two programs however. Both programs check that there is at least one argument to the program. The first program, however, only tries to open and loop thru the first argument. The latest program will loop thru all files. So, if we had invoked both programs with *prog file1 file2*, then the first program will just square the numbers in *file1,* while the second example will square the numbers in both files.

Elegant Solution for Common "ps" Problem

Suppose you want to list the active processes on your system. You would use the "ps" command:

```
$ ps


PID  PPID SIZE ENV  DS   Command
0254 0008 02db
0530 0008 0004
0535 8e7e 06fe 0000 0545 (SH) -L -0 C:/UNIX/BIN/SH.EXE -R 0
0c34 10ae 0010
0c45 26d1 0010
0c56 FREE 001e         480 bytes
0c75 0535 0438 0c34 0c75 (mouse.co)
10ae 0535 0055 0c34 10ae (vi.exe) \unix\bin\vi.exe
1104 10ae 15cc 0000 2111 (/unix/bi)  -c ps
26d1 1104 02a5 0c45 285d (ps.exe) \unix\bin\ps.exe


$
```

Now, suppose you are only interested in the process information for "vi". You could do the following:

```
$ ps | grep vi
10ae 0535 0056 0c34 10ae (vi.exe) \unix\bin\vi.exe
1105 10ae 15cd 0000 2112 (/unix/bi)  -c ps | grep vi


$
```

The problem is that you also get the entry for the "grep" process itself.

There is a simple, elegant solution:

```
$ ps | grep [v]i
10ae 0535 0056 0c34 10ae (vi.exe) \unix\bin\vi.exe

$
```

In regular expressions, brackets contain either-or options. So "[sz]ys" would match "sys" or "zys". If only one character is in brackets, as in "[v]i", then the regular expression simplifies to "vi" upon execution.

Thus, in our case, "grep" is simply looking for "vi", but the "ps" entry for the "grep" contains the original "[v]i", so we prevent a match.

Looking at specific lines in a large logfile

One day, a co-worker asked me for help. She was trying to look at a specific error message in a unix logfile that was too big to view with an editor.

She knew how to use *grep ERROR file* to display the lines that the error occurred on, but she needed to also see the lines on either side of the error.

I told her to first use *grep -n ERROR file* to return the errors with the line numbers.

Then she can use awk with each instance of the error to see the lines around it.

For example, if the grep showed the error ocurred on line 345, she could then use

awk 'NR>340 && NR<350' file

to see the 5 lines on either side of the error message.

Reversing a Text File

Here is an awk script called reverse_file, which reads in a text file, and prints the lines in reverse order.

i.e. if we have a file containing the following three lines:

foo

bar

bas

The output is:

bas

bar

foo

Here is the script:

```
#! /usr/bin/nawk -f
BEGIN {
        if (ARGC != 2)
        {
            print "Usage: reverse_file file"
            exit 1
        }
```

```
        }


    {

        store[NR] = $0

    }



    END {

            for (i=NR;i>=1; i--)

            print store[i]

        }
```

The script is pretty simple. There are three parts: a BEGIN section, a body section with no conditions, and an END section.

The BEGIN section is executed once when the script is run. It simply checks if there is an argument count of 2 (script name and one argument). If there is no argument, it prints a usage message and exits.

The body section has no conditions, so it is applied to each line in the file. It simply stores the line in an array called "store", that is indexed by the line count. So, for example, the 3rd line is stored in store[3].

The END section is run once after all input is read. It uses a for-loop to loop backwards thru the line count, and prints each line, from last to first.

Reversing the Unix ls command

list_reverse is an awk program that uses the unix "ls" command to list the files in the current directory, and to print the file names reversed.

For example, if the directory contains the files:

prog1.c

sample.txt

list_reverse will display:

prog1.c --> c.1gorp

sample.txt --> txt.elpmas

Here is the script:

```
nawk '
function reverse(a)
{
    b=""
    for(i=length(a);i>=1;i--)
        b = b""substr(a,i,1)
    return b
}

BEGIN {
while ( "ls"|getline)
```

```
        print $0" --> "reverse($0)

}'
```

The first thing to realize about this script is that, technically, it is a unix shell script that runs a nawk script, rather than a pure nawk script.

We do not use "!# /usr/bin/nawk" to tell unix to execute the whole program as a nawk script. Instead, it is a shell script, and we use *nawk 'program'* to run the nawk program.

We already know about awk BEGIN, body, and END sections. Now, we introduce awk functions.

In this case, we have a function *reverse* that takes an argument *a,* puts the reverse into *b*, and returns the value of *b*.   Since the *a* is a place-holder for whatever is passed into the function, *a* is a local variable and is only defined in the function. Any other variables, however, are global. Thus, the function could directly manipulate $1, for example, and the variable *b* could be referenced in other parts of the awk script.

This, in fact, is why the first part of the function sets *b* to empty - because it will have the value from the last time the function was invoked. So, in other words, variables that are referenced in a function are created the first time the function is invoked, and then have global scope for the life of the program.

The function then loops thru the length of the string *a*, and uses the substr function to build a reversed copy of the string in *b*.

The BEGIN part of the program uses "ls|getline" to get the list of files in the current directory, loops thru the file names, and prints the file name followed by its reverse (by calling the reverse function).

Celsius to Fahrenheit Conversion

Here is an awk program to convert between celsius and Fahrenheit temperatures.

Unlike most of my programs, this program is interactive. Once started, it interacts with the user at the command line, and accepts commands until the user quits.

Here is the run:

[513]-> cel_fahr

Current input set to: fahrenheit

enter q, f, c, or temp:

212

212 degrees F is 100 degrees C

Current input set to: fahrenheit

enter q, f, c, or temp:

rt

Current input set to: fahrenheit

enter q, f, c, or temp:

c

Current input set to: celsius

enter q, f, c, or temp:

0

0 degrees C is 32 degrees F

Current input set to: celsius

enter q, f, c, or temp:

q

In the run above, the user input is in black, while the displayed text is in green. Notice that when I type in a number, the system interprets it as either degrees C or F (depending on the input setting), and prints the conversion.

If I type "c" or "f", the input units are changed. If I type "q", the system quits. If I type anything else that is not a number (example "rt"), the program ignores it.

Here is the script:

```
nawk '
BEGIN {
        f = "fahrenheit"
        c = "celsius"
        choice = f
        while (x != "q")
        {
            print
            print "Current input set to: "choice
            print "enter q, f, c, or temp: "
            "read x;echo $x"|getline x
            close "read x;echo $x"


            if (x == "f") choice = f
            if (x == "c") choice = c
```

```
            if (x ~ /^[0-9]*$/ || -1*x ~ /^[0-9]*$/)

            {

               if (choice == f)

                   print x" degrees F is "5/9 * (x - 32)" degrees C"

                if (choice == c)

                   print x" degrees C is "x*9/5 + 32" degrees F"

            }

        }

    }'
```

Let's analyze the script. First, this script is completely in a BEGIN section, so it is a procedural program. We set the default choice to be fahrenheit, and then loop until the user enters a "q".

In the loop, we start by printing the menu, and then use getline to create a shell process which reads from the keyboard into unix variable x and then echos unix variable x into getline, where it is assigned to x in the awk program.

We then close the process so that, the next time we run the process, it will do a fresh read.

If the input is either "f" or "c", we set the choice.

Then, if the input is either a positive or negative number, we convert it from the input units to the other unit, and display the result.

Awk Day of the Week Program

Here is an awk script that returns the day of the week.

Here is the run:

[560]-> day_of_week

Usage: /usr/bin/nawk month day year

[561]-> day_of_week 09 11 2006

9/11/2006 was a Monday

Here is the script:


```
#! /usr/bin/nawk -f
BEGIN {

        DAY[1] = "Sunday"; DAY[2] = "Monday"

        DAY[3] = "Tuesday"; DAY[4] = "Wednesday"

         DAY[5] = "Thursday"; DAY[6] = "Friday"; DAY[7] = "Saturday"


    if (ARGC < 4)

    {

        printf ("Usage: %s month day year\n",ARGV[0])

        exit 1

    }


        m = ARGV[1]+0
```

```awk
    d = ARGV[2]+0

    y = ARGV[3]+0


    while ("cal "m" "y| getline)

    {

        if (NF==7) Sun = $1

    }


    dow = (Sun + 14 - d)%7

    if (dow == 0) dow = 7

    dow = 8 - dow

    printf ("%d/%d/%d was a %s\n", m, d, y, DAY[dow])

}
```

Let's see what is going on. The first thing to notice is that the whole program is in a BEGIN section - this means that the program will run as a procedural program, from top to bottom. This awk script will not try to open any input files and will not loop.

The first thing that the script does is initialize an array called DAY with 7 elements. For example, DAY[5] is equal to the string "Thursday".

Next, the script will exit with a usage message if the arg count is less than 4 (meaning 3 arguments plus the executable). So, we need to provide the script with 3 numbers: month, day, and year.

Next, we assign month, day, and year to the variables m, d, and y, respectively. We add 0 to each variable to get awk to convert them to numeric. **In general, you can append "" to a variable to force awk to treat it as a string, and add 0 to a variable to force awk to treat it as numeric.**

Now, we use getline inside a while statement to execute the unix command "cal m y", and loop thru its output.

Notice that the body of the while loop consists of only one if statement. This statement says that if the line has 7 fields, set the variable Sun equal to the first field.

Here is the output from running "cal 9 2006" in unix (note, I added the x's to preserve the spaces):

[565]-> cal 9 2006

September 2006

S M Tu W Th F S

xxxxxxxxxxxxx1 2

xxxxx3 4 5 6 7 8 9

10 11 12 13 14 15 16

17 18 19 20 21 22 23

24 25 26 27 28 29 30

So, after this while statement is done, Sun will be equal to 24.

Now, we do a little interesting math. To get the day of the week (dow), we add 14 to Sun (to get a number greater than the last day of the month, which is 30 in Sept), then subtract the day, and then use the % function to get the remainder from dividing the number by 7.

The remainder will be from 0-6. We then convert any 0 to 7, to make the numbers from 1-7. Finally, we subtract this number from 8 so that the days are in order, from 1 (Sunday) thru 7 (Saturday).

Two Awk Scripts for Calculating Compound Interest

Here are two awk scripts. The first one (compound) calculates compound interest on a lump sum. The second one (compound_add) calculates the total return when we deposit regular contributions, as opposed to a lump sum.

First script (compound):

The run:

```
[514]-> compound

Usage: /usr/bin/nawk principle rate time


[515]-> compound 100 10 4

Amount 100.00 compounded at 1.1000 for 4 yields:

1: 110.0000

2: 121.0000

3: 133.1000

4: 146.4100
```

The script:

```
#! /usr/bin/nawk -f
 BEGIN {
      if (ARGC < 4)
      {
```

```
        printf ("Usage: %s principle rate time\n",ARGV[0])

        exit 1

    }


    principle=ARGV[1]

    rate=ARGV[2]/100+1

    time=ARGV[3]

    printf ("Amount %.2f compounded at %.4f for %d yields:
\n\n",principle,rate,time)


    for (i=1;i<=time; i++)

    {

      principle *= rate

      printf ("%d: %.4f\n", i, principle)

    }

  }
```

Now, we will look at the second script (compound_add):

The run:

[517]-> compound_add

Usage: /usr/bin/nawk principle rate time

[518]-> compound_add 100 10 4

 Amount 100.00 added in each time and compounded at 1.1000 for 4 yields:

1: 110.00 (invested: 100)

2: 231.00 (invested: 200)

3: 364.10 (invested: 300)

4: 510.51 (invested: 400)

The script:

```
#! /usr/bin/nawk -f
BEGIN {

        if (ARGC < 4)

        {

           printf ("Usage: %s principle rate time\n",ARGV[0])

           exit 1

        }


        principle=ARGV[1]

        rate=ARGV[2]/100+1

        time=ARGV[3]

        printf ("Amount %.2f added in each time and compounded at %.4f for
%d yields: \n\n",principle,rate,time)


        for (i=1;i<=time; i++)

        {

           total = (principle + total)*rate

           invest += principle
```

```
        printf ("%d: %.2f (invested: %d)\n", i, total, invest)

    }

}
```

Notice that the two scripts are almost identical. The main difference is in the calculation, which is done as the script loops thru the time intervals.

In "compound", we simply keep multiplying principle by 1 + rate/100, to accumulate the value.

In "compound_add", we have to create a new "total" variable, so we can preserve the original principle value, so we can keep adding it in. In this case, we take the accumulation, add in a new principle, and apply 1 + rate/100 to the whole thing.

In the first example, we add in $100, and let it grow at 10% per period for 4 periods.

In the second example, we contribute $100 in each period, for a total of $400 invested. All contributions grow at 10%/period for however many periods that they are in the account.

Word Frequency

Here is a shell script called *word_freq* that uses *awk* to read in a file and return the count of each word. The script then uses *sort* to sort the words from highest to lowest frequency.

For example, if you have a file consisting of:

every good boy does fine

what a good boy am I

The program will return:

2 good

2 boy

1 what

1 fine

1 every

1 does

1 am

1 a

1 I

Here is the program:

```
nawk '
{
```

```
        for (i=1;i<=NF;i++)

        count[$i]++

}
END {

        for (i in count)

        print count[i], i

        }' $* |

sort -rn
```

The awk body is applied to each line, and it uses a for-loop to loop from 1 to NF (which is the number of fields on the line). It then uses the dollar sign to reference the contents of the field, and uses that to index an array called count.

So, for example, on the first line, $2 is "good", so count["good"] is set to 1. when the next line is processed, $3 is "good", so count["good"] is set to 2.

Then, after all the input is processed, the END section uses the for...in.. version of the for loop, which is used to loop thu the elements of an array. We then print out the word count, and the word.

In awk, when the array index is a non-numeric, the for...in loop returns the element in random order. Thus, we pipe the output into "sort -rn" (the "r" argument reverses the sort to go from higher to lower, while the "n" argument makes the sort numerical, rather than lexicographical).

Selecting the Most Recent File in a Directory

If you want to select the most recent file in a directory, you can use:

ls -rt | tail -1

The *ls -rt* will list the directory from oldest file to newest file. This command by itself is very handy if you are interesting in listing the most recent files in a directory with many files. This way, you can see the most recent files without scrolling.

Piping a command to *tail -x* will return the last *x* lines of output. so, *tail -1* will return the last line of output.

Together, *ls -rt | tail -1* will return the most recent file. Of course, you can always add qualifiers to the *ls* command, like *ls -rt *.log* to get only *.log* files.

you can feed this combination into another command, such as the *vi* editor, using back ticks (`).

So, the command *vi `ls -rt *.log | tail -1`* will guarantee that you edit the most recent log file in the directory. This is very handy if you are debugging a problem and running a program multiple times.

Unix Basic Calculator

Unix provides a basic calculator program: **bc**

(Like most unix utilities, the command name is simple and minimal).

The first lesson to using bc, is to always invoke it with **bc -l**. This is because, by default, the command does not load the floating point library. Here is an example of the difference in a division problem:

[668]-> bc

5/3

1

quit

[670]-> bc -l

5/3

1.66666666666666666666

qu

Maybe loading the floating point library was taxing to 1970's computers, but it is a non-factor today. (This shows how unix commands are so simple and robust, they never have to be modified). So, I made it a habit to always run **bc -l**.

As we can see from the example above, the bc interface is beautifully minimal - which makes it very handy. You just type bc -l, type math problems, press return, and get your answer. Type "quit" (or even just "qu") to quit.

You can use +, -, %, /, *, ^, and parenthesis. You also have functions like *sqrt()* (square root), *length()* (# of decimal positions), *l()* (natural log) and *e()* (exponential function). You can also use user-defined functions.

MAN Pages

In Unix, if you ever need help with any commands or options, just type "man command".

For example, *man ls* will return the manual pages for the ls commands. This way, you don't have to memorize all the options for each command.

On some systems, when you use *man*, the text comes up using the *more* utility (which displays text a page at a time). On some systems, however, the *man* pages are just scrolled onto the screen, so you won't be able to read them. If this is the case, then you should either redirect the command to a file (i.e. *man ls > ls.txt*) or pipe *man* to the *more* command (i.e. *man ls | more*).

Unix Change directory Command

In unix, the **cd** command is used to change directories. For example, *cd /tmp* will put you in the /tmp directory.

 Here are some tips/tricks for *cd*:

cd by itself *or cd* ~ will always put you in your home directory.

cd ~username will put you in username's home directory.

cd dir (without a /) will put you in a subdirectory. for example, if you are in /usr, typing *cd bin* will put you in /usr/bin, while *cd /bin* puts you in /bin.

 cd .. will move you up one directory. So, if you are /usr/bin/tmp, *cd ..* moves you to /usr/bin, while *cd ../..* moves you to /usr (i.e. up two levels). You can use this indirection to access subdirectories too. So, from /usr/bin/tmp, you can use *cd ../../local* to go to /usr/local.

 cd - will switch you to the previous directory. For example, if you are in /usr/bin/tmp, and go to /etc, you can type *cd* - to go back to /usr/bin/tmp. You can use this to toggle back and forth between two directories.

Awk Script to Sum Integers

I love elegant simplicity over brute force. An example of this is the formula for adding up consecutive integers.

This formula, $N*(N+1)/2$, is equal to adding up the integers from 1 to N.

No matter what language is used, programs that use this formula to add up integers will always use one calculation, while a loop would have to go through all the numbers. This means that programs using the formula will always execute instantaneously, even when adding up millions of integers.

Here, then, is the awk script for adding up the integers from 1 to N:

```
#! /usr/bin/nawk -f

BEGIN {

        if (ARGC == 2 )

        {

            n = ARGV[1]


                # The sum of numbers 1...n is n(n+1)/2

            sum = n * (n + 1) / 2

            print "The sum of 1 to "n" is "sum

        }


        if (ARGC != 2)

        {

            print "Usage: sums n "

            print " returns sum of 1 - n"
```

```
        exit 1

    }

}
```

Script to Sum Any Range of Integers

We just looked at an awk script for summing the integers from 1 to N, based on the formula N*(N+1)/2.

 After writing the above script, I then derived a general formula for summing the integers from M to N.

This is N*(N+1)/2 - M*(M-1)/2.

 The awk script "sumit" below will do both kinds of calculations. If you run *sumit 10*, it will give you the sum of 1 to 10. If you run *sumit 6 10*, it will give you the sum of 6 to 10.

```
#! /usr/bin/nawk -f
BEGIN {

        if (ARGC == 2 )

        {

            n = ARGV[1]


                # The sum of numbers 1...n is n(n+1)/2

            sum = n * (n + 1) / 2

            print "The sum of 1 to "n" is "sum

        }


        if (ARGC == 3 )

        {

            m = ARGV[1]
```

```
        n = ARGV[2]
    if (m>n)

    {

        print "First value must not be larger than second."
        exit 2

    }


        # The sum of numbers m...n is n(n+1)/2 - m(m-1)/2
    sum_m = m * (m - 1) / 2
    sum_n = n * (n + 1) / 2
    sum = sum_n - sum_m
    print "The sum of "m" to "n" is "sum

  }


if (ARGC != 2 && ARGC !=3 )

{

    print "Usage: sumit n "
    print " returns sum of 1 - n"
    print " sumit m n "
    print " returns sum of m - n"
exit 1

}


}
```

Awk substr function

Let's look at the substr function of awk.

This function has the form **substr(s, a, b)** and returns **b** number of chars from string **s**, starting at position **a**. The parameter **b** is optional.

Assume that we have a one line file called temp:

Every good boy.

Then, here are some substr examples:

nawk '{print substr($1,1,1)}' temp   returns E

nawk '{print substr($1,3)}' temp   returns ery

nawk '{print substr($2,3)}' temp   returns od

nawk '{print substr($0,7,2)}' temp returns go

Using Awk to Find Average Annual Interest Rate

Earlier, we looked at two awk scripts for calculating compound interest.

Now, let us look at the opposite problem. If we have a starting amount and ending amount, after X number of time periods, what is the average interest rate per time period? We can use awk.

For example, If we started with $4000, and had $5200 after 6 years, what interest rate did we average per year?

We can use:

```
nawk 'BEGIN {print (5200/4000)^(1/6)}'
```

to get an answer of 1.0447. So, we made about 4.5% a year for 6 years.

In this case, we are using the math principle that raising something to 1/N is like taking the Nth root.

So, 4000* 1.0447^6 = 5200.

Unix Date Command

The unix date command returns the current date and time stamp:

```
[560]-> date

Thu Oct 5 09:59:33 CDT 2006
```

You can customize the display by using a formatting string.

Some examples:

```
[561]-> date '+%m/%d/%Y'

10/05/2006


[562]-> date '+%m/%d/%y'

10/05/06


[563]-> date '+%m%d%y.%H%M%S'

100506.100131
```

The last example is great for creating unique log file names.
So you can do the following in your script:

```
DATE=`date '+%m%d%y.%H%M%S`

LOG=/tmp/programname.$DATE
```

and then redirect any messages to > $LOG

There are lots of formatting options for date. You can use *man date* to check out the manual pages.

Awk split command

Awk has a split command, which takes a string and splits it into an array, and returns the number of elements. The default separator is white space.

As an example, let us assume that a line in a log file consists of:

4/2/2003 11:23:18 This is a log entry with timestamp.

and we have an awk program like this:

```
{
   split($1,DATE,"/")
   n = split($2,TIME,":")
   print "Month is "DATE[1]
   print "Minutes are "TIME[2]
  print "Time has "n" parts"
}
```

Running the program against the log file line would result in the following output:

Month is 4

Minutes are 23

Time has 3 parts

Setting Default Values For Unix Shell Variables

The unix korn shell has a shortcut method for returning a default value for a variable that is not set, so that you do not need to use an *if* loop to check it.

For example, let us assume that the variable T is not set.

Then, *echo $T* returns nothing.

However, *echo ${T:-"not set"}* will return not set.

So, let us say that you write a script that takes an optional numerical argument. If the argument is not specified (i.e. $1 is not set), you want the argument to default to 2.

You could do

```
if test "$1" = ""
then
    VAL=2
else
   VAL=$1
fi
```

or you can just do

```
VAL=${1:-2}
```

Awk Script for 5x5 matrix

Here is an awk script that reads in a 5x5 matrix and prints the matrix, along with the sums of the rows and columns.

Given file rr:

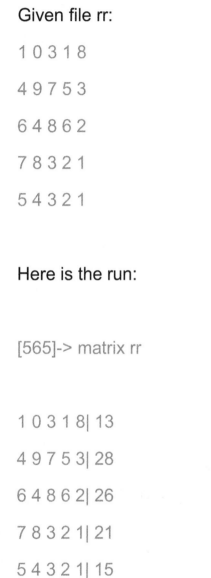

1 0 3 1 8

4 9 7 5 3

6 4 8 6 2

7 8 3 2 1

5 4 3 2 1

Here is the run:

[565]-> matrix rr

1 0 3 1 8| 13

4 9 7 5 3| 28

6 4 8 6 2| 26

7 8 3 2 1| 21

5 4 3 2 1| 15

----

23 25 24 16 15

Here is the script:

```
#! /usr/bin/awk -f

{

R=$1+$2+$3+$4+$5

print $0"| "R

C[1]+=$1

C[2]+=$2

C[3]+=$3

C[4]+=$4

C[5]+=$5

}

END {

print "------------------------------"

print C[1]" "C[2]" "C[3]" "C[4]" "C[5]

}
```

The script loops thru each line (row). For each row, it computes the total, then prints the row and total. Then, it adds each column element to a running total.

The END loop gets run after all the rows are processed. It prints the final column totals below each column.

Solving A Multi-Line Problem With Awk

Here is a problem that spans more than one line in a file.

Problem

Given a text file such as:

Part 1
  564 32718 976
  54 2345 987 50
  432 1 75
Section 2
  281 34 1290 345
  21 8 4 3

Create a script that outputs:

Part 1: 564 32718 976
Part 1: 54 2345 987 50
Part 1: 432 1 75
Section 2: 281 34 1290 345
Section 2: 21 8 4 3

 Solution

As we loop thru each line with awk, we will encounter two types of lines - either a header (like Part 1) or a content(like 564 32718 976).

If we encounter a header line, we need to store it. If we hit a content line, we need to print it, along with the current header.

We can describe the header line by this pattern:

```
NF==2 && $2 ~ /^[0-9]/
```

This will match any line "that has 2 fields and the second field starts with a digit from 0 to 9."

To store it, we can use the action:

```
{ prefix = $1" "$2 }
```

For a content line, it is sufficient to note that its first field is numeric (starts with a 0-9):

```
$1 ~ /^[0-9]/
```

In this case, we need to print the current prefix and the content line like this:

```
{ print prefix":"$0 }
```

Putting it all together, our shell script for solving the problem is:

```
#! /bin/ksh
nawk '
   NF==2 && $2 ~ /^[0-9]/ {  prefix = $1" "$2 }
   $1 ~ /^[0-9]/ { print prefix":"$0 }
     ' $1
```

Example of Awk Pattern Matching

Here is a problem-solution exercise that I wrote about 12 years ago, as another example of pattern matching:

Problem:

  Compose a script or command to print out the lines in a text file that contain "abc", and either "rst" or "xyz", but not "0.00".

Solution:

```
nawk '/abc/ && ( /rst/ || /xyz/ ) && $0 !~ /0\.00/' filename
```

The tricky thing here is that we must escape the period, otherwise it will match any character.

Solution2:

Now, when I wrote the above solution, notice that, for the 0.00 check, I used $0 !~ /0\.00/

The ~ and !~ are used when comparing strings with patterns. Since I'm checking the whole line, I can drop the $0 ~ and write just the pattern, like the other patterns (of course, I have to include the negation !):

```
nawk '/abc/ && ( /rst/ || /xyz/ ) && !/0\.00/' filename
```

Unix test command

The unix *test* command can test for various conditions, and then returns 0 for true and 1 for false.   Usually, *test* is used in *if...then* or *while* loops.

There are two ways of invoking *test* - either *test condition* or *[condition]*

Strings are compared with =, !=, >, and <.

For example, *test "$1" = "yes"* is true if $1 is "yes".

Numbers are compared with -eq (equal), -ne (not equal), -lt (less than), -le (less than or equal), -gt (greater than), -ge (greater than or equal to).

For example, *test $1 -lt 4* means that $1 is a number less than 4.

Here are some other conditions:

test -r file   True if file *file* exists and is readable.

test -w file   True if file *file* exists and is writeable.

test -x file   True if file *file* exists and is executable.

test -d file   True if file *file* exists and is a directory.

test -s file   True if file *file* exists and has a size greater than 0.

test -z string   True if string *string* exists is length 0.

conditions can be compounded with -o (or) or -a (and).

For example,

if test $SIZE -lt 5000 -o $DAY != "Sun" will be true if $SIZE is less than 5000 or $DAY is not equal to "Sun".

For more conditions, use *man test*.

Awk Regular Expressions

In Awk scripts, you can use regular expressions to match text. Regular expressions are encolsed in forward slashes (/).

In the pattern part of an awk script, the regular expression by iteself means that the pattern is checked against the whole record ($0).

For example, /jump/ {print $1} will print the first field if the line contains jump.

Regular expressions can be matched to strings by using the tilde (~).

For example, $0 ~ /jump/ {print $1} is equivalent to the statement above, while

$2 ~ /jump/ {print $1} will only print the first field if the second field contains the pattern.

Brackets allow alternatives in regular expressions. For example, /[Jj]ump/ {print $1} will print the first field if the line contains jump or Jump.

A ^ anchors the pattern to the start of the string. So /^jump/ {print $1} will only print the first field if the line starts with jump. It will not, for example, match parachute jump.

A $ anchors the pattern to the end of the string. So /jump$/ {print $1} will print the first field if the line is jump or parachute jump, but not jump out.

A * after a character or brackets means "0 or more", while a + means "1 or more".

So, /j*/ would match jump, banjo, and cook, but /j+/ would match jump and banjo, but not cook.

Example of Renaming Files in Unix

Problem

Write a script to automatically rename all files in the current directory
that have the ".txt" extension to the same name, with a ".doc" extension.

Thus, "foo.txt" becomes "foo.doc", "bar.txt" becomes "bar.doc", etc.

Solution

First, we use the unix's for-loop mechanism to loop through all
".txt" files, and perform some as yet undefined actions:

```
for i in *.txt
do
   actions
done
```

The above code will loop through all files with extension ".txt", one at a time, and
set i to the full name of the file.

Now, two actions are necessary. First, we must generate the new filename, then
we must rename(move) the original file to the new file.

To generate the new name from the old, we need only perform a simple
substitution.

This is a job for sed!

```
j=`echo $i | sed s/\.txt/\.doc/`
```

This line pipes the value of i into a sed command, which replaces the ".txt" with ".doc". This modified value of i is then assigned to j.

To rename the file, we simply execute:

mv $i $j

Putting it all together, we get the following shell script:

```
for i in *.txt
do
    j=`echo $i | sed s/\.txt/\.doc/`
    mv $i $j
done
```

However, my advice would be that, before you run any for loop that modifies files, you run a version which displays what you want to do, just to double check.

So, before you execute our script to actually move the files, I would substitute

echo $i $j for mv $i $j and run this loop to make sure you are moving the right files to the right extension.

Using Temporary Files in Unix Scripts

If you need to use one or more temporary files in a unix script, you should append $$ to the filename.

$$ returns the process id of the process that is running that instance of the script. This is important because unix is multi-tasking, and it is very possible for a script to be running multiple times, simultaneously.

Unless a temporary file has a unique name, there is the danger that simultaneous runs will overwrite the temporary file, causing problems.

For example, if your script used:

TMPfile=/tmp/stordata

The file will not be unique for different runs of the program. So, if the script is running two times simultaneously, both sessions will write to /tmp/stordata at the same time.

On the other hand,

TMPfile=/tmp/stordata.$$

Will be unique for each session. In the case of two users running the script simultaneously, the two processes that are running the script may be 1234 and 1476, for example. So, the first script will write to /tmp/stordata.1234, while the other writes to /tmp/stordata.1476.

After using the temporary file(s) in your script, you should clean them up by removing them.

This can be done by a line such as the following at the end of the script:

```
/bin/rm -f $TMP 2>/dev/null
```

Notice that we are using the -f option to *rm*. This is because *rm* sometimes prompts you if you want to remove the file. The -f overwrites this.

The other thing is that we are redirecting standard error to */dev/null*. This means we do not want to display any error messages from the *rm* on the screen.

Unix Find Command

The unix **find** command lets you recursively search a directory for files, and even run commands on the files as they are found.

The basic **find** command is:

find *dir*

This will return a list of all files and directories, from directory *dir* on down. For example, *find* . will return all directories and files from the current directory on down.

We can add the *-name* option to look for specific files:

i.e. **find /tmp -name "*.log"**

Will return all files with the *.log* extension that are under the */tmp* directory structure.

We can use the *-exec* option to run a command on each file that **find** finds.

In this example, we also use the *-mtime* option to only select files that have not been modified in a certain number of days:

find $log_dir -name "*.log" -mtime +14 -exec rm {} \;

This will find all *.log* files under the $log_dir directory that have not been modified in 14 days and, for each file that is found, the **rm** command will be run, and the {} will be replaced by the file name.

Whenever you use the -exec option, you have to end the line with a space and \;.

These are the main **find** options that I use. If you want to learn more, you can do a **man find** to see the manual pages.

Awk OFS parameter

In awk, OFS is the output field separator. By default it is a space.

This parameter is used by the print command when you separate strings by using a comma.

For example, if we have a test file consisting of one line:

burp boy orange

Then running the following script on the file:

```
nawk '
{
print $1,$2,$3
OFS="%"
print $1,$2,$3
print $0
}' $*
```

Will produce the following output:

burp boy orange

burp%boy%orange

burp boy orange

Notice that, in the first print, OFS is the space by default. So the fields are printed with a space in between them.

Then, we set OFS to be a % sign, and the next print statement outputs the fields separated by a %.

Finally, we do a print on $0 to illustrate the fact that $0 always preserves the original format of the line.

Adventure Game Written In Awk

I wrote a small text-adventure game in awk - just to stretch the perception of awk, and show that it can be used as a programming language.

This game is small, but gives a taste of the fantasy adventure games of the 80's - like Zork from Infocom.

In this adventure, you are in a cave complex, and need to find the hidden gold to win. The adventure lets you move around, search, pick up objects, and use them. It uses a menu instead of free-form entries.

Here is the awk code:

```
nawk '

function intro() {
print
print "You are a brave adventurer. You have entered a hidden"
print "cave just outside town, that is rumored to hold gold!"
print "To win this adventure, you need to get the gold."
}

function invent() {
if (coin || axe || sword)
print "You are carrying: "
```

```
if (coin) print "coin"

if (axe) print "big, rusty battle axe"

if (sword) print "small sword"

}


function cave() {

print

print "You are standing in a cave. Sunlight gleams behind you"

print "from the entrance. In front of you, is a wooden door."

print "You see an opening to the left, and one to the right."

print

invent()

print

print "What do you want to do? "

print

print "(o)pen wooden door"

print "go (l)eft"

print "go (r)ight"

print "leave thru the (e)ntrance"

if (sword) print "break door with your (s)word"

if (axe) print "break door with your (a)xe"

print "(y)ell Open Sesame"

print "e(x)amine area"

print "read (i)ntroduction"
```

```
"read x;echo $x"|getline x

close "read x;echo $x"

if (x=="o") {print "The wooden door is shut tight."; cave()}

if (x=="l") {deadend()}

if (x=="r") {cave2()}

if (x=="e") {print "You decide to quit. Goodbye!";exit}

if (sword&&x=="s") {print "your sword breaks!";sword=0;cave()}

if (axe&&x=="a") {

print "You chop down the door and find the gold!!"

print "Great job, bold adventurer!"

print "This is the end of this adventure, but"

print "you have a promising career ahead of you!"

exit;

}

if (x=="y") {

print "A band of evil goblins passing by the entrance"

print "hear you, enter the cave, and kill you"

exit;

}

if (x=="x") {print "You find nothing";cave()}

if (x=="i") {intro();cave()}

print "What do you want to do?";cave()

}
```

```
function deadend() {
print
print "You are in a dead end"
print
invent()
print
print "What do you want to do? "
print
print "go (b)ack"
print "e(x)amine area"
print "read (i)ntroduction"
"read x;echo $x"|getline x
close "read x;echo $x"
if (x=="b") {cave()}
if (x=="x") {print "You find a sword!";sword=1;deadend()}
if (x=="i") {intro();deadend()}
print "What do you want to do?";deadend()
}

function cave2() {
print
print "You are in another cave."
print "You can go back, or explore a niche to the left."
print
```

```
invent()

print

print "What do you want to do? "

print

print "go (b)ack"

print "enter (n)iche"

if (rubble) print "(s)earch rubble"

print "e(x)amine area"

print "read (i)ntroduction"

"read x;echo $x"|getline x

close "read x;echo $x"

if (x=="b") {cave()}

if (x=="n") {niche()}

if (rubble&&x=="s"&&!coin) {print "you found a coin!";coin=1;cave2

()}

if (rubble&&x=="s"&&coin) {print "you found a nothing!";cave2()}

if (x=="x") {print "You see a pile of rubble";rubble=1;cave2()}

if (x=="i") {intro();cave2()}

print "What do you want to do?";cave2()

}


function niche() {

print

print "You are in a niche."
```

```
print "There is a dwarf here!"

print

invent()

print

print "What do you want to do? "

print

print "go (b)ack"

print "(t)alk to dwarf"

if (!sword&&!axe) print "(f)ight dwarf"

if (sword) print "fight dwarf with (s)word"

if (axe) print "fight dwarf with (a)xe"

if (coin) print "(o)ffer coin to dwarf"

print "e(x)amine area"

print "read (i)ntroduction"

"read x;echo $x"|getline x

close "read x;echo $x"

if (x=="b") {cave2()}

if (x=="t") {print "The dwarf grunts";niche()}

if (x=="f") {print "The dwarf kills you";exit}

if (x=="s") {print "The dwarf kills you";exit}

if (x=="a") {print "The dwarf kills you";exit}

if (coin&&x=="o") {print "The dwarf takes the coin and gives you a

n axe!";coin=0;axe=1;niche()}

if (x=="x") {print "You find nothing";niche()}
```

79

```
if (x=="i") {intro();niche()}

print "What do you want to do?";niche()

}
```

```
BEGIN { intro(); cave() }
```

'

This is one of the longest awk programs that I have written. Notice that it is function-driven. I have created functions to give the introduction, and the inventory, and I have created functions for each room.

The awk program is kicked off by the BEGIN section, which runs intro() and cave() to put you in the first room.

Each object is represented by a variable of the same name (i.e. sword for sword) and is either 0 (off) or 1 (on), depending if you have the object.

Each function will print descriptions and gve options, depending on the setting of these boolean variables.

The inputting is done by using getline to run "read x;echo $x" to read from the screen and echo the response into awk. Then, a close is done so that the next getline will get fresh input.

WildCards for Unix Shell Commands

Let's look at some common wildcards you can use with unix commands.

For example, lets assume that the current directory has the following files:

proxy.txt
proxy1.txt
proxy2.txt
proxy11.txt
Proxy1.txt

Then let's use the *ls* command to demonstrate the differences between the wildcards.

* matches 0 or more characters.

So, *ls proxy*.txt* returns
proxy.txt
proxy1.txt
proxy2.txt
proxy11.txt

while *ls proxy1*.txt* returns
proxy1.txt
proxy11.txt

? matches 1 character.

So, *ls proxy?.txt* returns
proxy1.txt
proxy2.txt

while *ls proxy1?.txt* returns
proxy11.txt

[] matches 1 character from a range of characters.

So, *ls [pP]roxy1.txt* returns
proxy1.txt
Proxy1.txt

and *ls proxy[12].txt* returns
proxy1.txt
proxy2.txt

Searching for Special Characters in a File

I co-worker asked me to help him with a *grep* command. He wanted to use *grep* -*v* to return all lines in a large text file that did not contain the special character ï¿½

He told me that, using the unix octal dump utility (*od*), he found that this character was represented by the octal codes of 357 277 275.

Now, I tried to play around with these numbers but could not figure out how to generate the character. Then, I got the idea to cut/paste it from the instant message window (that he was communicating to me thru) to a unix text file. Then, I saw that unix represented it as \357\277\275.

I then solved it thru *awk*. I realized that I could store it in a string variable:

```
c = "\357\277\275"
```

Then, I can use the *awk index* command, which returns the position of a substring inside another string (it returns 0 if the substring is not present).

So,

```
if (index($0,c)) print $0
```

Would print the current line if the character was present anywhere on the line.

Since he wants the lines **without** the character, I added a ! in front of the index:

if (!index($0,c)) print $0

Putting it together, I got the following command to return all lines in a file without
ï¿½

nawk '{c="\357\277\275";if (!index($0,c)) print $0}' filename

Running Multiple Unix Commands On The Same Command Prompt

Let's look at some ways to run unix commands on the same command prompt.

```
$ cmd1 & cmd2 &
```

This will run both commands in the background, in parallel.

```
$ cmd1; cmd2
```

This will first run cmd1, and then cmd2. It is the equivalent of running cmd1 on the command prompt, pressing return, and then running cmd2 at the next command prompt.

```
$ cmd1 && cmd2
```

This will run cmd1 first. If cmd1 runs successfully (return code 0), then cmd2 is run.

```
$ cmd1 || cmd2
```

This will run cmd1 first. If cmd1 runs un-successfully (non-zero return code), then cmd2 is run.

Comparing Time On Two Unix Servers

You can check that the time on two unix machines are synchronized by logging into machine1, and then simultaneously running the *date* command on machine1 and machine2, using *remsh* (remote shell):

$ date; remsh machine2 date

This will return the current date/time from both machines, and you can see if they are in sych.

I actually once had a production problem that was caused by one unix server having its timestamp out of synch by 25 seconds. The machine that was running 25 seconds fast was running a program that was waiting for a response from a program running on the second machine (that had the proper time).

The first program was supposed to wait for up to 2 minutes, and then timeout. We noticed that it started timing out a lot. We first thought that there was some problem with the second program, or with the communication between machines.

But, then we figured out that the clocks were out of synch, and so the first program was timing out when the second server still had 25 seconds in which to respond.

Unix shell Script Here-Document Function

The Unix shell has what is called a "here-document" function which allows you to put input under a command, instead of in a separate text file, and feed it into the program.

This is done by placing a "<<" and a character string after the command. Then, every line after the command is interpreting as free-form text to be fed into the command, until a line is hit that has the character string.

For example,

```
awk '{print $1}' <<!
jack be
nimble jack be
quick.
!
```

Would behave exactly like

```
awk '{print $1}' < file
```

where the file would contain:

```
jack be
nimble jack be
quick.
```

Awk Script to Combine Lines in a File

Problem: We have a text file containing individual records spanning multiple lines. We want to combine them into one line each.

For example, given:
Name: John Doe
Age: 32
Zip: 60324
Name: Jane Doe
Age: 34
Zip: 54930
Name: Skippy
Age:134
Zip:23456

We want:
Name: John Doe Age: 32 Zip: 60324
Name: Jane Doe Age: 34 Zip: 54930
Name: Skippy Age: 134 Zip: 234556

Solution:

We want the following Awk script:

```
/Name/  {
        print d
        d=""
       }


  { d=d" "$0}

END { print d}
```

When a Name: line is hit, this script prints the current value of variable d, and then clears it. Then, for all lines (including the Name: line) the variable d is built up.

Then, the END statement gets executed to print the last record.

Unix Stream Editor

The Unix stream editor (*sed*) is useful for editing streams of text. You can either pipe the text into *sed*, or else give a file name - in which case, *sed* works on the file.

In all cases, *sed* does not change the original text, but sends the modified text to standard out.

Sure, I could just use *awk* but, for some tasks, its just easier to use *sed*.

Some examples:

sed 4q   Prints the first 4 lines of the file.

sed 's/yes/no/'   Substitute "no" for the first occurance of "yes" on each line.

sed 's/yes/no/g' In this case, substitute "no" for all occurances of "yes".

sed 's/yes/no/2'   Substitute "no" for the second occurance of "yes" on each line.

Finding Duplicates in a File

If you have a text file, you can find lines that are duplicated by running

```
sort file | uniq -d
```

By default, the uniq command takes a sorted list and prints each line once. If you add the -d option, it only prints lines that occur more than once.

For example,

```
file1
-------
hello
lemon
lemon
hello
```

if you run uniq -d file1, you get:

```
lemon
```

This is because only lemon occurs more than once in a row.

So, to get all duplicates, we run sort file1 | uniq -d, which returns:

```
hello
lemon
```

Running Multiple Unix Commands

Let's look at some ways to run unix commands on the same command prompt.

$ cmd1 & cmd2 &

This will run both commands in the background, in parallel.

$ cmd1; cmd2

This will first run cmd1, and then cmd2. It is the equivalent of running cmd1 on the command prompt, pressing return, and then running cmd2 at the next command prompt.

$ cmd1 && cmd2

This will run cmd1 first. If cmd1 runs successfully (return code 0), then cmd2 is run.

$ cmd1 || cmd2

This will run cmd1 first. If cmd1 runs un-successfully (non-zero return code), then cmd2 is run.

Unix Change Directory Commands

In unix, the cd command is used to change directories. For example, cd /tmp will put you in the /tmp directory.

Here are some tips/tricks for cd:

cd by itself or cd ~ will always put you in your home directory.

cd ~username will put you in username's home directory.

cd dir (without a /) will put you in a subdirectory. for example, if you are in /usr, typing cd bin will put you in /usr/bin, while cd /bin puts you in /bin.

cd .. will move you up one directory. So, if you are /usr/bin/tmp, cd .. moves you to /usr/bin, while cd ../.. moves you to /usr (i.e. up two levels). You can use this indirection to access subdirectories too. So, from /usr/bin/tmp, you can use cd ../../local to go to /usr/local.

cd - will switch you to the previous directory. For example, if you are in /usr/bin/tmp, and go to /etc, you can type cd - to go back to /usr/bin/tmp. You can use this to toggle back and forth between two directories.

Complex Global Substitution in Unix Text files

A co-worker asked me to help him change all bfx* files in a directory.

Inside each file, he wanted to change all instances of:

/2007

with:

/`date +%Y`

In other words, he wanted to remove the hard-coded 2007 and have unix automatically run the date function to compute the current year.

Here was my solution:

```
for i in bfx*
do
sed 's/\/2007/\/\`date +%Y\`\/' $i > tmp
mv $i $i.bak
mv tmp $i
done
```

Searching through Directories in Unix

Here is a script called "search" that will allow you to search through a hierarchy of directories for files that contain a word or phrase:

```
echo "The pattern is found in these files:"
find . -exec grep -il "$*" {} \;
```

You could type in, for example, "search green" or "search will be going". In the first case, it will return the names of files that contain "green". In the second case, it will return the names of files that contain the phrase "will be going".

Search works because of the find command. The unix find command searches directories recursively, and it has the -exec option, which allows you to specify a command to be run on any file that is found.

The format of the -exec option is: -exec command options {} \;

command and options are just the command name and any options. The {} are place holders for the file name. Find will replace them with the name of each file that it finds. The \; is used to signify the end of the command.

In this case, we are giving a grep command as the argument to the exec option.

Note that search is case insensitive so "search green" would return files with "green", "Green", "GREEN", etc.

For case sensitive searches, I have a script called searchcase. The only difference in searchcase is that the "i" in the grep is removed.

Using Unix Commands on Web Pages

We can parse web pages with unix tools by first using the lynx text browser to retrieve the page.

For example, in this case we are using the lynx browser to return an Oncall page (which lists which support people are on call), and then extracting the Primary support person:

```
LD_LIBRARY_PATH=$LD_LIBRARY_PATH:/usr/local/lib
URL="http://www.oncallPage.com/contacts/"

/usr/local/bin/lynx -dump $URL | grep Primary | sed 1q
```

First, I am setting the LD_LIBRARY_PATH variable because, at least on my system, lynx needs this setting.

Then, I create a string variable called URL which holds the URL of the web page I'm interested in.

Finally, I call lynx. The -dump parameter tells lynx to return the formatted page to standard out.

At this point, it is simply a text stream which we can edit like any other text stream. Here, I am grepping any lines that contain "Primary", and then using sed 1q to return just the first instance.

Using AWK to Generate SQL from File

Here is a unix script that will read in a text file containing customer ids, Old Template Names, and New Template Names.

The script will use awk to generate sql statements that can be run in oracle to rename the templates from old to new, for each of the companies.

This script would come in handy when we have a whole file full of templates to change, and don't want to write the sql by hand.

The interesting thing is that we use sprintf to store the apostrophe in the variable sq. This way, we can output apostrophe's, which normally cannot be embedded in awk.

```
#! /bin/ksh

nawk -F\t '

BEGIN { sq=sprintf("%c",39) }

{
custid = $1
old = $2
new = $3
printf("UPDATE TEMPLATES SET TEMPLATENAME = %c%s%c\n
",sq,new,sq)
printf("WHERE TEMPLATENAME like %c%s%c and custid = %c%s%c;\n",
sq,old,sq,sq,custid,sq)
}' $*
```

Calculating the Previous Month in Unix

Here is a unix shell script that calculates the previous month.

Here is the run:

[576]-> last_month

Today is 10/10/2006

Last month was 9/2006

First day of last month was 9/01/2006

Last day of last month was 9/30/2006

Here is the script:

```
day=`date +%d`

month=`date +%m`

year=`date +%Y`

echo "Today is $month/$day/$year"


lmonth=`expr $month - 1`

if test "$lmonth" = "0"

then

lmonth=12

year=`expr $year - 1`

fi

echo "Last month was $lmonth/$year"
```

```
lday=`cal $lmonth $year |awk '$0~/[0-9]/ {print $NF}'|tail -1`
echo "First day of last month was $lmonth/01/$year"
echo "Last day of last month was $lmonth/$lday/$year"
```

The first part of the script uses the unix date command to retrieve today's day, month, and year. We print today's date.

'

Next, we use the korn shell's *expr* command to subtract 1 from the month. If the month becomes 0, then that means that this month is January, so we wrap the date to December of the previous year. We print out the previous month and year.

In the third part, we retrieve the last day of the previous month, and then print the first and last days of the previous month.

The tricky thing here is how we retrieve the last day. We run the unix *cal* function to return last month's calendar. We pipe it into an *awk* command, which prints the last field from each line. We pipe this to *tail -1*, which returns the last line of the awk output.

This whole pipeline is enclosed in back ticks (`) so that we can assign the final output to the variable **lday**.

Let's look at this, using the 9/2006 *cal* entry:

```
[578]-> cal 9 2006
September 2006
```

```
S M Tu W Th F S
1 2
3 4 5 6 7 8 9
10 11 12 13 14 15 16
17 18 19 20 21 22 23
24 25 26 27 28 29 30
```

The above *cal* output would go to *awk*, which would output:

```
S



16
23
30
```

This would be piped to *tail -1*, which would return 30.

Processing Multiple Files Through Awk

Problem

Given an arbitrary number of text files, compose an awk script to search the first 20 lines of each file for a pattern, and then print each matched line, along with its filename.

Solution

The solution makes use of two awk values: FNR and FILENAME.

FNR is the line number expressed RELATIVE to the current input file, while NR is the line number RELATIVE to all input. Thus, if file1 (containing 20 lines) and file2 were the inputs to awk, NR for line 1 of file2 would be 21, but FNR would equal 1.

FILENAME contains the name of the current input file being processed. Thus, when lines from file1 are being evaluated, FILENAME="file1". When line 1 of file2 is reached, FILENAME becomes "file2".

Thus, the solution to the problem is:


```
nawk 'FNR<=20 && /pattern/ {print FILENAME":"$0}' files
```

Unix Script to Capitalize First Letter of Word

A friend at work asked me for help with an interesting unix problem.

He wanted his script to look at the first argument passed on the command line ($1).

If the first letter of the argument was capitalized (i.e. Boy or DOG), he wanted to assign the argument to variable *y* as it is, with no changes.

If the first letter was lowercase (i.e. boy or dOG), he wanted to capitalize the first letter of the word before assigning it to *y*. But, he only wanted to capitalize the first letter. He did not want to capitalize the whole word. So, *boy* would become *Boy*, not *BOY*. For *dOG*, it would become *DOG* since the *OG* was already uppercase.

So, here is my solution:

```
typeset -u first=`echo $1|nawk '{print substr($1,1,1)}'`

rest=`echo $1|nawk '{print substr($1,2)}'`

y=$first$rest
```

I am using a variable called *first* to hold the first character of $1. I am using the awk substring function to return the substring of $1 that starts with position 1, and is 1 character long.

I used *typeset -u* to denote that variable *first* stores uppercase only. This means that anything assigned to *first* will be automatically capitalized.

I am using the variable rest to hold the rest of $1. I used the awk substring function to return the substring of $1 that starts in position 2. I did not specify a length, so it automatically returns the characters up to the end.

So, for example, if $1 was *sunset*, then substr($1,1,1) returns *s* and substr($1,2) returns *unset*.

Finally, I assign *$first$last* to *y*, so that *y* now holds $1, with the first character guaranteed to be uppercase.

Pulling Sections From An XML File Using AWK

Recently, I had to pull all mt100 records out of a file that was written in XML format. So, I needed to pull out anything between mt100 and /mt100 tags, while ignoring the rest of the file.

I used the following awk program:

```
/mt100/ {writ=1}

writ==1 {print $0}

/\/mt100/ {writ=0}
```

Remember that an awk program consists of pattern-action combinations. Each line of input is processed and, if any patterns evaluate to true, the corresponding action is performed.

In this case, awk will ignore lines in the file unless one of three conditions are met:

1. The line contains the pattern mt100. If this occurs then a variable called writ is set to 1.

2. If writ is 1, then we print the current line. All awk variables are initialized to 0.

3. The line contains pattern /mt100. If this occurs than writ is set to 0.

So, writ is a flag. It starts off as unset, then gets set whenever we hit the mt100 tag, and is unset when we hit the /mt100 tag. Whenever writ is set, lines get output.

Thus, we end up pulling all mt100 blocks out of the file.

Unix Sort Question

A co-worker asked me for help on a sort issue.

He had a file with the format of an alpha part and then a numeric part.

Here is an example:

abf 11111

abc 11111

abde 11111

abc 11112

He wanted the file sorted only using the alpha part, and he wanted lines with duplicated alpha parts removed.

So, using the example input file, the output would be:

abc 11111

abde 11111

abf 11111

He had tried to use the *sort* and *uniq* commands, but was having trouble.

Here is the solution that I gave him:

sort –u –k 1,1 file

Let's analyze this command.

The *-k 1,1* option causes the sorting to be done on the first to the first field. In other words, only use the first field for sorting.

The *-u* option eliminates the need to pipe the output to *uniq*. Coupled with the *-k 1,1* option, it removes lines that are duplicates only in the first field - which is what we want.

Unix Script to Find Difference From Two Time Stamps

Here, we will find the difference between these 2 time stamps (assume they are from the same day):

"5:02:02"

"5:19:59"

Here is the script:

```
T1='5:02:02'

T2='5:19:59'


h1=`echo $T1|cut -d: -f1`

m1=`echo $T1|cut -d: -f2`

s1=`echo $T1|cut -d: -f3`

x1=`echo "$h1*3600 + $m1*60 + $s1"|bc -l`


h2=`echo $T2|cut -d: -f1`

m2=`echo $T2|cut -d: -f2`

s2=`echo $T2|cut -d: -f3`

x2=`echo "$h2*3600 + $m2*60 + $s2"|bc -l`


if test $x1 -lt $x2
```

```
then

diff=`echo "$x2 - $x1"|bc -l`

else

diff=`echo "$x1 - $x2"|bc -l`

fi


echo "diff of $h1,$m1,$s1 and $h2,$m2,$s2 is $diff seconds"
```

We are storing the time stamps in T1 and T2. Then, we use the cut command to extract the hour, minute, and seconds fields for each time stamp. We then calculate T1 into seconds and store it in x1. We calculate T2 into seconds and store that in x2.

Then, depending on whether x1 or x2 is bigger, we subtract the smaller number from the bigger number by piping the subtraction into the unix basic calculator (bc).

We give bc the -l option to load the floating point library. Since we are only adding integers we don't need the library, but I always give the command, because there is hardly any overhead.

Using Unix Shell Script to Build Java Classspath

Scenario: You want to run a java program from a shell script. Before you invoke the *java* command, you want to build the CLASSPATH vaariable dynamically with all the jar files in a certain directory (denoted by $java_dir).

Solution:

```
for line in $java_dir/*.jar

do

CLASSPATH="$CLASSPATH:$line"

done
```

This *for loop* will cycle through each file in the directory $java_dir that has a ".jar" extension.

During each pass, the variable "line" is set to the full pathname of the jar file. We add the jar's pathname to the CLASSPATH.

Using Awk To Generate Random Coupon Code

Here is an awk script I use to generate 100 random 8-character coupon codes.

Each character has 62 possibilities (a-z, A-Z, and 0-9). This means there are 8^62 possible coupon codes.

```
BEGIN {

s="abcdefghijklmnopqrstuvwxyzABCDEFGHIJKLMNOPQRSTUVWXYZ0123456789"

srand()

for (i=1;i<=100;i++)

{

code=""

for (j=1;j<=8;j++)

code = code""substr(s,int(rand()*62)+1,1)

print code

}

}
```

Let's analyze the script. First, we set string *s* to hold all 62 possible characters.

Next, we call *srand()* to seed awk's random number generator. We left the argument blank, so that the current date is used for seeding.

We now loop 100 times, because we want to output 100 coupon codes.

In this loop, we first set the coupon code back to the empty string. Then, we have an inner loop that executes 8 times to build the code. Finally, we print the code.

Notice the command in the inner loop. This command uses the random (rand) function. Since rand() returns a number greater or equal to 0, and less than 1, we multiply it by 62 and use the integer (int) function.

This will return a number between 0 and 61. Why? Because $int(0*62) = int(0) = 0$ and $int(.999...*62) = int(61.99...) = 61$.

We then add 1 to the result to get a random number from 1-62. We then use this result in the substr function to randomly pick a character.

Splitting a Unix File into Smaller Files

Let's say that we have a large unix file. For example, a text file called *my_list* with 100,000 lines.

We need the data contained in smaller files with no more than 1000 lines each.

We can use the unix *split* command:

split -1000 my_list

This will create 100 files in the current directory that each contain 1000 lines from my_list. Since we did not specify a name for the output file, the files will be named by an *x*, followed by two letters of the alphabet (from *aa* to *zz*).

So, for example, the first 1000 lines of *my_list* will be in file *xaa*, the next 1000 lines in *xab*, the next 1000 in *xac*, etc.

If we had specified an output file name like this:

split -1000 my_list my_list

then the output files would have been *my_listaa*, *mylistab*, etc.

The Split Function in Awk

Awk has a split command, which takes a string and splits it into an array, and returns the number of elements. The default separator is white space.

As an example, let us assume that a line in a logfile consists of:

4/2/2003 11:23:18 This is a log entry with timestamp.

and we have an awk program like this:

```
{
  split($1,DATE,"/")
  n = split($2,TIME,":")
  print "Month is "DATE[1]
  print "Minutes are "TIME[2]
  print "Time has "n" parts"
}
```

Running the program against the logfile line would result in the following output:

Month is 4

Minutes are 23

Time has 3 parts

Accessing Unix Command Output in Awk

You can run a unix command through awk, and then access the command's output within the awk script.

The trick is to use: "cmd"|getline

The first call to "cmd"|getline will open it as a pipe and fetch the first line of output. Each subsequent call will fetch the next line of output. If there is no output, it will return empty.

For each line, $0 will be automatically assigned to the whole line, and the fields ($1, $2, etc) will be assigned by breaking up on the whitespace pattern.

You can use this neatly in a while statement:

```
while ("cmd"|getline)

{

}
```

Here is an example to print the environmental variable settings:

```
#! /bin/nawk -f

BEGIN {

while ("env"|getline)

{

print $0

}
```

}

This will run the "env" command in a unix shell and it will keep looping until there are no more environment variables. Each line will be printed by the print command.

A Formal Way To Parse Command Lines in Shell Scripts

For unix scripts that get executed by lots of other users, I like to make them user friendly by allowing arguments to be passed in any order.

For example, let's say that I created a script called **cube** that takes four parameters: three values for the cube's dimensions (height, width, and depth) and a flag to make it a die (i.e. have the sides numbered 1-6).

For quick and dirty scripts, I would just read in the arguments in order. For example, I might assign $1 to height, $2 to width, $3 to depth, and $4 to flag.

So, if a user ran **cube 3 4 5 1**, I would create a 3x4x5 cube that was a die.

If I wanted to make the script user friendly, I would specify the parameters **-height**, **-width**, **-depth**, and **-die**, where the first 3 params would take an argument.

Let's further clarify that the height is the only required parameter. If the width or depth is omitted, it would be the same as the height. If **-die** is not provided, then the cube will not be a die.

My shell script would start with two functions: **Usage** and **parseArgs**.

The **Usage** function simply prints out the possible arguments and whether they are optional (i.e. in brackets):

function Usage

{

echo "Usage: cube -height height [-width width] [-depth depth] [-die]"

}

The **pargeArgs** function initializes a heightcheck variable to 0, because height is a required field. Then, as long as the first argument ($1) exists, the while loop will execute. The while loop uses a nested case statement to identify the parameter, and then does a shift to shift all arguments to the left (so $2 becomes the new $1). If the parameter takes an argument, then $2 is accessed and an extra shift statement is done.

```
function parseArgs

{

heightcheck = 0

while [ -n "$1" ]

do

case "$1" in

-height) height="$2"

heightCheck=1

shift

;;

-width) width="$2"

shift

;;

-depth) depth="$2"

shift
```

```
      ;;

   -die) die=1

      ;;

   esac

   shift

done

# make sure we got a height on the command line...
if [ $heightCheck = 0 ] ; then
Usage
exit 2
fi

}
```

After these functions, the main script will start. First, we will check for the arguments by calling parseArgs with the arguments to the script:

```
# Parse Command Line
parseArgs $*
```

Next, We will set the defaults. **${a:-"b"}** returns a if a is set (assigned a value) or else it will return b:

```
# Set defaults if these args
# were not set on command line.
width=${width:-"$height"}
depth=${depth:-"$height"}
die=${die:-0}
```

After this, you write the rest of your script.

Running Unix Commands on Directories With Too Many Files

Today, a co-worker sent me an email asking for help.

He was trying to run **grep pattern * > /tmp/tmpfile** in a directory containing 240,695 files and he got the error "ksh: /bin/grep: arg list too long".

He thought the limitation was in **grep** and so asked me to provide him with the equivalent **awk** script. I told him that it was not a **grep** problem. The issue is with too many arguments on the command line - so the problem would happen with **awk** also.

You simply cannot put 240,695 arguments on a command line.

The solution is to use a for loop, so you are actually running the command 240,695 times with only one argument:

for i in *

do

grep pattern $i >> /tmp/tmpfile

done

Extracting Initials In Awk, Part 1

Someone once asked me for help.

They had a file *file1* containing first and last names. They wanted to output the initials to a new file *file2*.

So, if *file1* contained "charlie brown", the script had to write "cb" to *file2*.

Here's my solution:

```
awk '{print substr($1,1,1)""substr($2,1,1)}' file1 > file2
```

Extracting Initials In Awk, Part 2

After I gave the solution above, I was asked how to refine it so that the script wrote each set of initials with the number of times it occurred.

So, for example, if the file was:

charlie brown
orphan annie
chuck barry

The output was:

cb1
oa1
cb2

Here is my solution:

```
awk '{

initial=substr($1,1,1)""substr($2,1,1)

INITCOUNT[initial]++

print initial""INITCOUNT[initial]

}'
```

The first line sets a variable initial to be the initials (i.e. cb).

The second line sets an associative array called INITCOUNT that is indexed by initial. The code increments the value of INITCOUNT by 1. So INITCOUNT["cb"] is 1 the first time the initial is "cb", the next occurrence sets it to 2, etc.

Generating Random Numbers In Awk

In awk, you can generate random numbers with the *rand()* function.

Like most number generators, you need to "seed" the function (i.e. provide an initial value for the mathematical process), otherwise the function will return the same values.

You can seed the awk random generator by calling *srand()* in the BEGIN section of the awk program. By not providing an argument, it defaults to using the current date / time as the seed value.

The function returns a value *v*, where $0 <= v < 1$. This means that *v* can be a value in between 0 and 1, and it can be 0, but it can't be 1. In other words, *v* can be 0, 0.12, 0.65, 0.999, etc.

So, the way to generate a random number in awk from *M* to *N* is to use the formula *value = int(rand() * N) + M*.

For example, if you want to simulate a dice roll, you need to generate a random number from 1 to 6. This means that the random value can be 1, 2, 3, 4, 5, or 6. You would use int(rand() * 6) + 1.

Let's analyze it:

1. rand() will return a number from 0 to .9999...

2. Multiplying this value by 6 yields a number from 0 to 5.9998...

3. int() will round it down to the nearest integer, thus resulting in a number from 0 to 5.

4. Adding 1 yields a number from 1 to 6.

In the same way, a simulated coin toss (2 values) would be int(rand()*2)+1.

Using the Unix Dot (.) Operator to Run a Shell Script in the Current Shell

In unix, there is the dot operator. The syntax is a dot (period), followed by a space, and followed by a shell script:

. script

Why would you use the dot operator?

Normally, when you run a shell script, it executes in a child shell. Once the script completes, the child shell goes away and you are returned to the command prompt on the original shell. This means that the **scope** of the script doesn't apply to the invoking shell.

In other words, if your script changed the directory or set some variables, those changes won't be reflected after the script ends.

Using a dot space in front of the script means that the scope of the script is the same as the invoking shell.

For example, let's say that you are currently in the /usr directory and you run the script **go_tmp**, which changes the directory to /tmp.

If you run **go_tmp** then, after the script ends, you will still be in /usr.

If you run **. go_tmp**, then you will be in /tmp after it runs.

As another example, suppose you have a script set_java_classpath, which modifies your CLASSPATH environment variable so that you can run java programs. You will need the dot operator (i.e. run **. set_java_classpath**) so the new path is still there after the script ends.

The dot operator is also used a lot in shell scripts that need to call other scripts (like subroutines).

Sending Email From a Unix Script

Sometimes I need my unix script to email the output to a mailing list.

Here is how I do it:

1. I set a unix variable called MAIL_LIST that holds all the email addresses in a space separated list.

MAIL_LIST="john.doe@acme.com bob_jones@somewhere.org"

2. I set a variable SUBJ that holds the subject of the email.

SUBJ="Daily Report For "`date`

3. Instead of sending the output of the script to standard out, I send it to a temp file

4. At the end of the script, before exiting, I use /usr/bin/mailx to email the output.

cat $TMP| /usr/bin/mailx -s "$SUBJ" $MAIL_LIST

Customizing Your Unix Ksh Environment with .kshrc

You can modify the .kshrc (note the dot because it is a hidden file) file in your home directory by adding the following four entries (highlighted in **bold**):

alias -x ll='ls -l'

umask 002

stty erase "^H" kill "^U" intr "^C" eof "^D" quit "^\\" susp "^Z"

PS1="
**\$PWD **
`hostname`:[\!]-> "
export PS1

The first entry set an alias of "ll", so "ll" could be run like a command. It would do the long list function (ls -l).

The umask sets it so that files are created with a default permission of rw-rw-r-- and directories are created with drwxrwxr-x.

The stty line sets the terminal characteristics, so that his unix window's backspace key will work.

Finally, it sets the main command prompt(PS1) to always display the current directory, the machine name, last command process, and a -> for entering the command.

For example, if you were currently in the /etc directory, and your unix machine was called "donut", your command prompt would look like:

/etc
donut:[583]->

Note: Make sure that your .profile file in your home directory calls .kshrc, so that it is automatically loaded every time you log in to unix.

How To Use Multiple-Word Arguments in Unix Scripts

Did you know that unix command line arguments can be more than one word? You can group text separated by spaces into a single argument by surrounding the text with quotes.

For example, what are the differences between these argument lists?

boy girl

boy dog girl

"boy dog" girl

In the first example, we have two arguments: boy and girl. In the second example, we have three arguments: boy, dog, and girl.

In the third example, we have two arguments: boy dog and girl.

Awk Script to Generate an HTML Page With Randomly Labelled URLs

Here is an interesting awk script I created.

It reads in a file of URLs and then generates an HTML page containing links to each of the URLs. Each link will be labeled with a random number.

I used this script (and the page it generated) to do some testing with people I recruited off of Craigslist.

Here is the script:

BEGIN {srand();print "[html]"}

{

print "[a href=\""$0"\"]URL "NR*(int(rand()*62)+41)"[/a]"

print "[br]"

}

END {print "[/html]"}

Note: the [and] 's above need to be replaced with <>.

The first things to look at are the BEGIN and END statements. They are each run once - the BEGIN before the file is read in, and the END after.

The BEGIN statement prints the html tag and seeds the random number generator. The argument to srand() is empty, so we use the date/time for the seed. This way, we won't get the same random numbers every time the script is run.

The END statement prints the /html tag.

The two print statements will be executed for each URL in the input file.

The first one will output the link. The rand() function will return a number that is greater than or equal to 0 and less than 1. So we can write this as $0 <= n > 1$

So, in other words, the lowest value returned by rand() is 0 and the highest is .9999...

Next we are multiplying rand() by 62 and using the int() function. This will result in an integer from 0 to 61. Then, we are adding 41. This means that the random label used for the link will be from 41 to 102.

In general, the format *int(rand()*x)+b* results in a random number from *b* to *x+b*.

So, *int(rand()*6)+1* replicates a 6-sided die, and generates a random number between 1 and 6.

The second print statement outputs a newline.

Using Awk to Generate HTML and Java Script

In the previous example, we used awk to read in a file of URLs and generate a static HTML page with links to each URL. The links were labeled with a random number from 41 to 102.

In this script, we do the same thing, except that, for each URL, we write javascript which will randomly build the link 5% of the time, at runtime.

So, we are using random numbers twice. First, in the awk script itself to create the labels for the links. Second, we were writing the javascript random function to the output, so that this random function is run every time the page is loaded in a browser.

Let's use an example to make it clearer. Pretend we have a file with 1o URLs. If we run the awk script form the last post, the output will be an HTML file that displays all 10 links, each one labeled by a random number.

If we run this same file on the script below, we will have an HTML page that runs a javascript routine for each link to decide whether or not it gets displayed. Each link only gets displayed 5% of the time. So, this HTML file will display from 0-10 links every time it is loaded into the web browser.

Here is the awk script:

```
BEGIN {srand();print "[html]"; apos=sprintf("%c",39)}

{

print "[SCRIPT LANGUAGE=\"JAVASCRIPT\"
TYPE=\"TEXT/JAVASCRIPT\"]"

print "var i = Math.round(100*Math.random());"

print "if (i<=5)"

print "{"
```

```
print "document.write("apos"[a href=\""$0"\"] URL "NR*(int(rand()*62)+41)
[/a]"apos");"

print "document.write("apos"[br]"apos");"

print "}"

print "[/script]"
}

END {print "[/html]"}
```

Note: the [and] 's above need to be replaced with <>.

Notice the apos constant. In the BEGIN block, we set it equal to the apostrophe.
This way, we can insert apostrophes for the javascript, without awk processing
them.

Calling Unix Commands From Within Awk: system vs getline

Inside an awk script, there are two ways in which you can interface with the operating system: system() and getline.

system() is good if you want to just run a command, and don't need any results back.

getline can be used when you want your awk program to return data back into the awk script.

Some examples:

ret_code = system("sort file1 > file2")

while("grep true file"|getline x)

The first example sorts a file, and then stores the return code in the ret_code.

The second example is running a grep command in unix. It is running the command through getline. Here, the getline statement is inside a while loop. The loop will keep looping until there is no more data from the grep. Each call to the while loop results in x holding the latest data from the grep command.

Creating csv Files From Unix When the Data Has Commas

Here is a problem that has occurred a few times for me:

I run a query on a unix database using sqlplus from a shell script. I then save the results in an csv (comma separated value) file and load it into Excel. What I find is that some rows have extra columns.

The reason it happened is that some data contains commas.

Here is a way to prevent this:

1. Extract the data with a % (or other symbol) separating the data.

i.e. select field1||'%'||field2||'%'||field3 from table

2. Use sed (unix stream editor) to remove all commas, and then convert the %'s into commas:

cat sqlfile | sed 's/,//g' | sed 's/%/,/g'

Then, your columns should line up in excel because the data will no longer contain commas.

Using uuencode to Mail Attachments From Unix Shell Scripts

At work, I frequently have to do queries on an Oracle database, and send out the results in a spreadsheet.

If the report can be done with SQL alone, I usually do the report on my PC using TOAD (Tool for Oracle Admins and Developers). TOAD lets you save the results as an excel spreadsheet.

If, however, the report was complex where it required manipulating the output through unix shell / awk scripts, or I wanted to automate the report, I had to run the query from unix through sqlplus. If I then mailed the report from unix, the data would be in the body of the email. This isn't good if the report had a lot of columns.

I recently found a solution. It is a unix utility called uuencode, which let's you send data as an attachment. By sending the report as a csv (comma separated values) file, the email will appear in Outlook on my PC with an attachment that will open in Excel with one click.

Here are two ways to use it (assume that the report was saved in a text file called rptfile, and all data are separated by commas):

uuencode rptfile report.csv | /usr/ucb/mailx -s $SUBJ $MAIL_LIST

(cat bodyfile; uuencode rptfile report.csv) | /usr/ucb/mailx -s $SUBJ $MAIL_LIST

The first way sends an empty email with report.csv as an attachment. The second one also sends an email with report.csv as an attachment, but the email also has the contents of bodyfile in the body of the email.

Removing Carriage Return Line Feeds (CRLF's) From Text Files in Unix

In unix, each line in a text file ends with a line feed. Windows text files, however, end each line with a carriage return and a line feed.

Normally, when you ftp a text file between Windows and unix, the end of line characters get converted. Sometimes, however, the carriage return and line feed get translated into Unix. This can happen, for example, if the FTP is set to binary mode before the file is sent.

When a unix file has both a carriage return and a line feed, it will display a control M at the end of each line. You can remove them in the vi editor:

1. vi the file.
2. Type colon to get a search line.
3. Type 1,$s/ctrl v ctrl m/$

Control v is needed to "escape" the entering of control-m.